Words from the Mouth of the Wolf

Meg Elisabeth

The Conrad Press

Words From the Mouth of the Wolf
Published by The Conrad Press in the United Kingdom 2025
Tel: +44(0)1227 472 874
www.theconradpress.com
info@theconradpress.com
ISBN 978-1-917673-09-9
Copyright ©Meg Elisabeth 2025
All rights reserved.
Typesetting and Cover Design by: Levellers
The Conrad Press logo was designed by Maria Priestley.
Printed and bound in Great Britain by Clays Ltd, Elcograf S.p.A.

Contents:

ARTEMIS

APHRODITE

PSYCHE

PYTHIA

THALASSA

THEMIS

To my grandparents,
Who continue to hope my poems will one day be more positive.
To my grandparents,
Who live inside my heart, with whom I will someday share my poetry.

I
ARTEMIS

Home

Pine- I smell pine
It is wrapped around me
Enveloping my senses
I am in a forest, a wood
Perhaps by a lake
My fingers skim over the fresh grass
The tickle pulls a giggle from my throat
Clouds swarm overhead
It is dark
But the smell of pine centres me
I am safe here
In a world of green

It Can Fix Itself

The cold, grey-and-white fur looks soft
It looks comfortable and oddly warm
But it is uncared for
Un-stroked
Unclean
Unloved
With a tentative hand I reach out to feel the coat
I am careful and slow and quiet
But just as my fingers graze a soft ear, the creature
                                  snarls
It snaps at me with vicious, sharp teeth
I draw back my hand and glare at the animal
Its position is tense and predatory
Its wide green eyes are guarded
Its lips are peeled back and its fangs are bared
The Wolf will not let me close
The Wolf will not let anyone close

Help Me

I want to be pried
And pushed
And prodded
And banged
Until someone finds a way
To open me up
Because I don't know how
To do it on my own
I've been permanently closed
For as long as I can remember
So please break me
And make me cry
Help me to feel
Help me find my emotions

Foolish Desire

I envy my reflection
for the simple life she leads
Running from mirror to mirror
trying to keep up with me
She has no wants or worries
no thoughts that turn to dreams
She lives a blissful ignorance
far away from me
She only exists when I need her
to analyse my sleepy smile
It turns my eyes blurry
emerald as the Celtic Isle
The image of some ancient queen
she wears them like fine jewels
They gleam with sharp knowledge
that others mistake as coldly cruel
My reflection is real, though
a person of her very own
I am her only friend
I think she likes it just so
She wanders along beside me
even when I don't know she's there
Smiling at me from windows
waving her arms up in the air
When I see her, it makes me smile

though envy broils within me
I wish I were a reflection
Left to wander alone and free
Existing always beside my clone
unbound by the pressure of reality
Flitting along as we walk her life
together until the last of her days
I'd happily die without a care
stoking the flare of our final blaze

Do You Hear That?

Do you hear that?
It's the sound of us growing apart
A hum in the distance growing fainter and fainter

Do you hear that?
It's the sound of your betrayal
It bangs abusively inside my bruised heart

Do you hear that?
It's the sound of me leaving you behind
The pretty peals of victory bells and trumpets

Do you hear that?
I didn't think so.
It wasn't for your ears anyway

Migration

If the world was reversed
And I was Happiness
Watching a young woman
Stumble around desperately
As she searched for me
In all the wrong places
After those who claimed to love her
Callously drove me away
For years on end,
I would travel across space and time
Battling oceans and deserts
To be by her side
And reassure her I exist

She deserves me in the life
I had never meant to leave
In the first place

I Am Too Small

The god Neptune -
Whom the Romans
Reviled for fear
Of his ever-changing
Temperament, his
Vast, unpredictable
Power - he has always
Been my companion,
My master in times
Of reflection, of
Paradise. I love and
Fear him the way I
Have been told my
Whole life to love and
Fear another. Neptune
Is unworthy of my
Loyalty, I offer it to him
Despite his many sins
I cannot defy him,
I am too small

I Will Not Be Purged

I cannot cry
So, I only feel
Behind a mask of stone
I cannot cry

Delusions of Grandeur

There are colours in my head
That don't belong there
There are faces in front of me
I've never seen before
They follow me wherever I go
Relentless in their pursuit
They tell me they've known me
All my life, that they are my friends
I do not trust their silken voices
The perfection of their forms
They cannot possibly be human
But they carry such beautiful colours
As they remain two steps behind me
I cannot escape the taunting
Of their promises, too good to be true
Or their declarations of love
I know I cannot trust a word they say
But, God, do I want to anyway

Goddess of Cowardice

The sky is a blurred mass of clouds
The sea is grey and brewing a storm
The world feels angry
I am frightened by the vastness of its power
It reminds me too harshly
Of my own insignificance
Even when the world is at peace
I am no match for its tender touch
One gentle breeze could blow me to pieces
I am too small and I am too fragile
The human existence is too full of fear
I wish to be unafraid
I wish to be powerful
I wish to be fearsome
I wish to be godly
One day the world will tiptoe around my wrath

ADHD

Undiagnosed, unnoticed by people
Who were never qualified to read the
Signs, to read between the lines and
Trace the past, the present, the future
Parts of me that can only be explained
By a four-letter label that I always
Wished for as a child and realised might
Be real once I turned seventeen, a
Different name to explain more than
"Anxiety" ever, ever could and it's still
Undiagnosed because by its very
Definition I am sure, I am certain it is
Me, and yet I cannot bring myself to ask
Not because I fear it, no, I would embrace
It, I already have, I simply cannot help
But procrastinate getting the help that
Will help me stop procrastinating

Surgery

You shall find me at Epidaurus
Incubated in some great hall
Dreaming about the rotten
Fragment of my body that must
Be removed in order to cure
This pain - at least, in the dream-
World this is so; Asclepius waits
For me in my vision, a demanded
Price already falling from his
Lips as I find him sequestered
In the corners of my sleeping mind
His tongue is forked like a snake's
His eyes shine golden and kindly
I will pay his price, I will give thanks
I will be cured at his sanctuary

Atalanta

In the forest I found a lion
She was washing in some stream
Her golden fur gleaming and
Wet, wind-swept
I knew she was wild, I hoped
She was free
And when she turned her amber
Eyes and looked at me, I knew
She was special
Never had a lion ever seemed so
Human, so wise
I knew she would not hurt me
So, I peeled off my clothes and
Joined her in the cool water
We bathed together in the sun
Almost Mother, almost Daughter

II

APHRODITE

Orpheus & Eurydice

His song was sweet enough to sway the Earth
For her, his lovely wife, he would make the world
                              bow
Even the King and Queen of all things dead
Could not resist the lull of his lilting music
He could trick any enemy and gain many friends
With only an instrument in his hand and poetry on
                              his lips
But even his fairest tune could not conquer
                              mortality
Nor could it raise the dead and buried
His sweet voice failed him in his time of greatest
                              need
Now his heart is gone forever, rotting among the
                              ghosts
Far from the Dead King's palace,
And even further from her divine husband

Pinkish Dreamworld

I am laying in a field of roses
It floats like an island atop a broad lake
Surrounded by miles and miles of flamingos
Their fuchsia feathers drift above me on a phantom
                              wind
Their beaks dip into the rippling pink waters
My cheeks are flushed with sleep and my lips taste
                              of strawberries
I am in Aphrodite's world
Riding to heaven on a candy floss cloud

A Love that Spans Universes

There is a part of me that is lost
A chunk of my heart that has broken away
A slice of my soul that has travelled through time
        and space and landed with you
I carved it out myself,
After long hours spent nestled within your quiet
        words
I ripped that piece from my chest and hurled it
        across my world to you
I hope you have it now, that it sits preserved in a
        pretty jar by your bed
Cherished and watchful
I was glad to part from that sliver of self, though I
        am jealous of it for finding you
But I will willingly live this half-life,
Forever grateful that somewhere, somehow, I am
        with you

Un-Listened

There were lilies in your hand when you stood in my doorway
And carnations sit tenderly in a high vase by my bed
You planted peonies and put them in a pot on my windowsill
Loved by the sun and befriended by the orchid beside them
In the field where we lay you picked me daisies and made me a crown
You found a dandelion and tucked it gently behind my ear
When I walked down the aisle it was covered in roses and fallen petals
And a lily was pinned to your jacket, a reminder of that first bouquet
But I told you time and time again, and you never heard
Tulips are my favourite flowers

Us Inside My Head at Night

Hanging lights
Like wisps of cobwebs
Illuminating patterns
The colour of ice that
Seem so incredibly
Delicate

Flickering dreams
Like dandelion seeds
Surfing winds that
Drop them carelessly
In minds so intangibly
Hopeful

Dangling love
Like crystal raindrops
Heavily resisting the
Force of gravity that
Wants them to shatter
Before they can be
Caught

Worlds Apart

From where I sit in my armchair
A universe away from you
I can't help but fall in love
Your few, sweet words have ensnared me
The tender hazel of your gaze excites me
A galaxy away from your touch,
I desire you

From where I've left my armchair behind
And crossed worlds to fall together
I cannot help but despise you
Your cold, harsh words unravel my heart
The mocking grey of your stare cripples me
A whisper away from your fingertips,
I loathe you

I am content to love you in my world,
And to hate you in yours

Drowning

I was treading your water
'Til my muscles turned sore

Your currents strengthened
The more I struggled to swim

By the time I gave up
And turned back to shore
You sent a riptide to grab me
And pull me back in

Stuck in a whirlpool
Of your instability
My feet could barely
Touch the ground
And my lungs were full
Of polluted sea

Far from the sand
And no one around
To hear my cry for help

You almost drowned me

Severed

I sacrificed my power
So that I could have your heart

I wish I'd never thrown it away
I want my magic back, now

But I can't turn time without it
And you won't turn it for me

I'll Take Anyone

There is a girl over there
With olive skin and night-time hair
She watches me as I watch her
I want to ask her something, anything at all
I think she knows I'll never dare

There is a boy across the hall
As beautiful and he is tall
I wonder if he'll spare me a glance
With his eyes that shine like liquid honey
But he doesn't notice me, not even at all

There is someone far beyond this world
With shadowed eyes and dark hair curled
He is too far to touch with my hands
So, I settle for sending him my heart
It trembles beside him, adorned and pearled

First Love, Worst Love

I dream of you
Once every few months
Your face pops into my imagination
On some kind of cycle
My mind refuses to let you go
No matter how many years have passed
Since I loved you

When I dream of you
It makes me wonder
If you might be it
The one I'll find again in years to come
A soulmate
The right person, loved at the wrong time
It's a foolish thought

My dreams of you
Haunt me for days afterwards
I see your face in people I don't know
All the self-doubt you gave me
It becomes heavier
You have so much power
From miles and years away
I hate you for it

A Jaundiced Eye

And in the months after me
You hopped between girls
Like stones on a lake
Your 19-year-old charm
Lending to your conquest
While I was stuck at school
Spending six months
Fruitlessly begging one
Boy to make me his
My 17-year-old arrogance
Couldn't hide my inexperience
Behind the experience
You had given me so ruthlessly
And while you've remained at large
A thorn in someone else's side
My cuts have barely healed
The barbs you forged to my skin
Have only just begun to dull
A blend of gleaming blood and rust
It seems endlessly cruel
That you should go on
To find romantic success
While I spend six years wilting
Digging out my festered pieces
Which are still better and kinder
Than any piece of you

I Don't Like Boys Who Make Me Cry

Thalassa lives deep within me
She desperately wants to escape
To trickle out slowly through all my orifices
I'm tempted to allow it
To let her pour out of me in a thousand tears

The Fates prevail: she runs down my face
Staining my cheeks black and bitter
I feel her on my lips
And my tongue can't help but steal a lick
She tastes of salt and sadness

Thalassa wants to drown me
She chokes me with sobs as she breaks from her cell
Leaving a thousand tears in her wake
But I'm grateful to her for freeing herself

Thank you for emptying me

A Masterpiece

I always thought I liked brown eyes
And maybe I do
But yours are electric
A vast sky of blue
Like a deeply lit ocean
They shine with great light
Its spark almost blinding
Uncomfortably bright

I always thought I liked brown hair
I must've been wrong
'Cause yours was spun golden
Like wheat carved from song
It pulls me in
With its glow like the sun
A bond between souls
That can't be undone

I always thought I liked people
So different from you
I know it was foolish
To think it was true
Your light has bewitched me
And stolen my heart
Together we'd make
Such beautiful art

Love Dance

And he said "move with
your whole body
The one you have been told
all your life is too short, too
small, too clumsy
Move like the flamenco dancers
who twirl their wrists and
slap their thighs
Move like the ballerinas who
stretch their arms and *tip tip tap*
on their toes
Swish your hips and bend your
knees - use every precious inch"

I could not bear to tell him
that I cannot move like them,
not at all
'Cause nobody ever wanted
to see my body move that way
before

III

PSYCHE

Private Dreams in Private Places

The door closes with a light thud,
And within seconds a book is in my hands,
Open to its marked page
I dive into the words, into the story and the world
In that place I am finally free
I am alone and endlessly content

My escape is temporary,
Crudely interrupted by a light knock on my door
I pull myself from the pages,
And reality returns long enough for me to answer
I'm reading! I say angrily and hear footsteps recede
They don't dare disturb me in my private territory

The space is precious:
That line between reality and fantasy
I walk it bravely and wildly when I am alone
It is my balance
For in public, I am just a girl
But in private, I am a girl with a sword

Song of My Heart

There is music in my soul that can't stop playing
Its rhythm follows the hollow beat of my heart
Giving it beauty and depth with a chiming tune
The emotion in me dictates its melody

That sweet music is my most faithful companion
Found only in the furthest well of my being
Holding my heart in its lyrical hands
It will follow me through light and dark
Through life and death, pleasure and pain
It will guide me through my immortality

June Hazel

I know you not in life, yet you nest in my heart
A heavenly quarter of my lonesome being
Made through your muse, your mouthpiece, your
                                            art
Watched by your hazel eyes, alive but unseeing

And though your house is so far from mine
That we can never in this time truly meet
I've seen your presence play seek with life's line
When my father's tears you deign to greet

Though your talents I cannot admit to possess
Nor your sweet hazel eyes I know once were alight
So deep in my soul breathes your tender caress
When I look to the sky as I bid you goodnight

I have dreams that take place in a world unlike ours
Where we live all alone beneath Fate's falling stars

Balance

It frightened you to hold
Something so heartbreakingly precious
In your scarred, unworthy hands
Hands that have done such terrible things
Hands that have burned and bled and
Stabbed and tortured and strangled
You tell yourself that something so pure
So beautiful and new and so close to
Life should not be touched by such hands
But though your hands are marked with pain
They have done as much good as they have done
                            bad
Your hands have warmed and worshipped
They have held and comforted and wiped away
                            tears
In the scars atop them and within them
Lie countless stories, both worthy and unworthy
Your hands are as neutral as life and death
Your hands are fair and just and cruel
In them, anything can be safely held

The Fate of Odin's Poets

There is blessed Mead in my veins
It has turned my blood to gold
And painted my tongue swift
Until my words are rhyming
And my eyes are bleeding wonders

There is cursed Mead in my veins
It has poisoned my life with debt
And spilled gilded blood on your altar
Until my voice has died and immortalised
And my bones are burning in golden flames

Paper Thin

An albatross
Dragging spirit and soul
Leashed, unfed
Of hollow shape and
Rotting heart
Tinged cerulean and mustard
Pulled and ripped over miles
Pierced by shards of ivory
And scattered bone
Weighed and splayed
Feasted upon by vultures
Who pluck out a heart
A liver, a kidney

An albatross
Dragging lung and lung
Alone, unbreathing
Crumpled and twisted
Spat on with blood that
Gleams violet and glacial
Lugged across the surface
Of the full moon
Crying, scraping over
Knives and instruments
Dropped and discarded

At the feet of no one
Who does not feast

Unmade and Made Again

There's a place I go
Seven times each week
When I want to escape
And leave this world behind

It beckons to me night and day
Singing lullabies of comfort
That sweep me into epiphanies
And teach me how to breathe

I go there as often as I can
And let it wash away my fears
Sometimes it takes days or years
To reconcile myself with who I am
When I come back home

If only I could escape forever
I would leave in a heartbeat
And never look back
I was never meant to belong here

Born Green

In the car
Surrounded by nature
Foliage scratching at my chin
Floral perfume filling my senses
My body buried in leaves
Soil at my feet
Listening to my mother
My grandmother
Talking about the garden
Laughing in the rear-view mirror
At the reflection of me
Sprawled between two hydrangeas
Dove-white and dusty pink
I lean my cheek against the scratching leaf
I let in a sniff of flowery scent
I wiggle my feet against the soil
Inside this box of metal,
I am one with nature
I am conversing with the Earth
I am halfway home

The Mother of Lyricism is Unforgiving

I am a child of Erato
Her lyrical honey runs through my veins
Her sweet words flow from my pen
She presides over every inky stroke
And I pray to her before I write each poem
Lest she take her gift away

Preserve Me

If I die tomorrow
Do not search for me
In the sunsets
You will not find me there
Instead, you'll find me
In the comforting smell
Of a well-loved book
Or of black ink freshly spilled
I'll linger in the scent
Of pollen in the June-time air
And the bright orange petals
That wrap around the stem
Of a newly sprouted tulip
I will not smile down
From far in the sky
But from the world around you:
The sounds of a violin
Played by someone
Who never practised enough
And the voice of a girl
Who talks too fast
For her dad to understand
I'll hover in the zesty tang
Of breakfast juice
Or the sugary taste

Of anything too sweet to bear
In the comfort of my chair
Or the familiar warmth
Of a sisterly hug
You'll be sure to find me
I'll live on in my favourite things
If only you remember
To look for me there

The Mystery of Meg

it is difficult
to consolidate
my identity
when i do not
quite understand
which parts of
me are *me*

am i that which
i let you see?
or am i the
things i am not
brave enough
to say and do?

am i the thoughts
that circle
my mind
but never leave
my mouth?

do the jokes
i think of
off the cuff
represent my

innermost
self?

is it my opinion
or the opinion
of others
by which i
should define
myself?

am i my dreams?
am i my desires?
am i even *me*
at all?
does *me* exist
in the way
that i imagine
she does?
is she asleep
when i am,
too - or does
she lie awake
at night
thinking on
philosophy
and politics
and poetry?

who is she?
who is *me*?

who am i?

Grey

And they said that life was worth living
But she didn't see how
Why
What for
There was no life she had to live
No fun
No adventure
No catastrophe and no solution
A mundane life is not a life worth living
Not to her
But she cannot escape the monotony
The melancholy
She has no way to burst from this shell
To counter this spell
So, she must waste away
She does not want to die
But she does not really want to survive
She is not happy here

Fickle, Childish Curiosity

Once, late at night
When I was a child
I asked Jack why
He had cursed me so
Why talent did slip
Through my fingers
As easily as my care
Why my dedication
My determination
Never seemed to linger
Longer than it took
To realise I had no
Natural gift, I was
No masterful doer
Always, there seemed
To be, someone just
Slightly better than me

Jack looked at me kindly
Eyes owl-bright and
Darting, and told me
His touch was no curse
But a blessing that filled
Its selected with curious
Passion and fickleness

He smiled as though
This should explain
Away my doubt and
Expose my meek gratitude
But I could not see or
Believe there might be
A positive in 'fickle'
I remained unassured
With a pouting attitude

Upon seeing my
Hesitance to accept
This mercurial fate
Jack let out a chuckle
With a pat to my head
He told me one day
When I'd grown I'd
Understand better
That people who
Might tell me his
Touch made me lesser
Had simply forgotten
The truth of his
Childish call to fun
'A Jack of all trades is
A master of none, but
Oftentimes is better
Than a master of one'

I Am Mercurial

Small Mercury
You drift so close to
The sun whose

Burning, burning touch
Could wipe away
All trace of you.

You play with
Fire; you are as reckless
As the god they named

You for all those
Years ago:
Another world, another time.

You have yet to burn -
But a mercurial temperament
Is nothing light, nothing neglectable.

Already you have been
Struck: littered with
Deep craters the size of

Earthly trucks.

You are volatile and
Untrustworthy with your

Own well-being.
For now, gravity keeps
You in check -

But should it falter,
What's to stop
You from plunging

Recklessly towards
That bright sun and
Burn, burn, burn.

Amnesia

I inked my memories
onto paper like letters
Bottled and placed
gently onto the sand
Watched until an
ashy wave has washed
them away
Lest someone steal them
before they can reach you

Beneath the surface the
bottle is bumped and
jostled
Passed over fish scales
and coral reefs
Spurted with octopus
ink that slides off slowly
as the bottle is smashed
against a rock
The elements descend,
smearing my inked
reveries with salted water

Far from the distant
shore where torn and

sunburnt pages rest
among the remains of
a bottle green crystal
ornament, I feel my
memories smudge and
drown and dry sideways
I am worn, I am remade

IV

PYTHIA

Cryptic

Let me tell you a story
Don't rest your eyes
This isn't the kind of tale
You want to fall asleep to
You'll want to be awake
To listen to my words
They might tell tales
But they only teach truths

Keep your senses alert
Remember carefully
Every intonation matters
Each letter holds power
The meaning is yours to decide
My stories do not dictate
They guide and shape

Use my words to find yours
This is not a tale for the future
Do not recount it,
Through generations to come
It is not yours to speak
Your story lives between my words
So, listen with intent
And let me tell you a story

Platonic Soulmates

I placed a pot of gold and your feet, then pulled
        out my paintbrush
And drew a rainbow in the gloomy sky that leads
        from you to me
I hid another treasure at its end, tucked in the folds
        of my heart
There's a map in your hand that will guide you
        through the rain
But I have no doubt you'll find the path, because
        you always do
No one knows the way to my heart better than you

Burns Night

On the twenty-fifth day that housed my birth
Three solemn women sat by a distant hearth
Where they wove fabled threads with silent
                              tongues
'Til my life's fated path was well and done
They wove not with yarn nor with wool nor with
                               string
But with tears that speak and words that sing
They threaded with dreams and silver-lined clouds
With thoughts that grey and whisper too loud
Each muse and each lyric that they entwined
Were intended for me to weave wonders in kind
For that twenty-fifth day, it has always been known
Is the one that true poets would claim as their
                               home

Common and Ugly

In a meadow early this morning
Walking beside my dog
I came across the prettiest flower I'd ever seen
Tall and proud, petals in the shade of
A colour I had no name for
Yet undiscovered
It hurt to pluck it from amidst the weed-like grass
But my hand moved before I could tell it 'no'

I walked an hour with that flower
Tenderly cradled against my breast
Away from the curious sniffs of the dog
Protected from the vicious summer breeze
By the time I was home, it was missing just
One petal: a fine achievement
With tentative care, I gave it room on my
                              windowsill
The only plant under my observation
I'd never been one to bring the outside inside

The day spilled slowly by
Like thick honey dribbling from its wooden dipper
My thoughts drifted on occasion to that piece of
                              natural perfection
Sitting idly in a jar half-filled with water

I knew its beauty might fade, but I prayed
It might last a little while longer, if only so I could
                              show it
To my mother, my father when they came back
                              home

By mid-morning, its colour was muted
No longer unknown, but some common shade of
                              purplish blue
Bruised like blood risen to the skin's surface
By lunch, its head hung a little limply
Grieving the loss of its roots
Its sisters in the meadow of grass and weeds
By three o'clock, two more petals had fallen
And the flowerhead dangled precariously
Reaching for the window as if it might escape the
                              melancholy
Of my inorganic bedroom

My parents are home now
But my perfect flower is gone, replaced by this
                              dying thing
I mourn the loss of its beauty, its vivacity
Wishing I could go back and unpluck it
I show them the jar, water half empty
Thing drooping
I mirror its doleful expression
'What a lovely find,' my mother tells me

'A wildflower, so rare around here,' says my father

I hear the pity in their voices
I hear the lies
But when I look up, I see such sincerity in their faces
They gaze upon the thing in the jar
With the same awe I felt that morning in the meadow
Oh, wonder! Oh, joy! The flower has re-blossomed
It has come back to life and-

But no
What good actors they are
When I look at the jar, the thing is as dull as ever
The colour even more faded
The droop comically pronounced
Barely three petals still adorn its long-suffering stem
'I have never seen such an unusual colour,' they say
'I cannot think what to call it'
They gaze at the weed as if it holds some great answer
I look at it and see only questions
I look at it and see only death
I look at it and see beauty warped by time, an illusion

I Didn't Ask to be the Queen of Me

We are the rulers
Of our own lives

There is no use
In waiting for
Divine intervention
To steer us

I wait, anyway
Unsure of my fate
As I waste life away
Writing poetry that
I might never even publish

An Image of the Future

When I close my eyes, I see a cottage
Not the witchy sort, but the *Miss Honey* kind
It has a thatched roof and is trimmed with ivy
Even with my eyes shut, I can smell its sweetness
Fresh, spring air blows gently against my eyelids
                              and
the wild tulips that wreath the garden kiss my skin
When I walk inside, a hearth sparks warmth in my
                              heart,
and although my eyes aren't open, I can still see
                              you there
You're waiting for me, smiling softly with dimpled
                              cheeks,
reaching for me the way a child reaches for her
                              mother
Rustic, wooden stairs lead me invitingly through
                              the home,
and I can see memories treasured everywhere I step:
                              hung
lovingly in white-trimmed frames against auburn
                              walls
Even the cold-hearted wife of deepest December
                              would be
soothed by this darling home that lives behind my
                              closed eyes

Bitter Gratitude

sometimes it's like
i don't deserve
to feel sad or
to complain about
my emotions
because i know
i have so much
to be grateful for
because my life has
been so full of wonder
so full of opportunity

my thread was spun
golden and brassy
when placed in the light
but put it under
a microscope and
you will see fraying
where brilliant paint
has come away to
reveal the thin
grey string beneath

Can a Bike Tell the Future?

By a house on my road
I saw a bike
With big, round wheels
And sleek blue handlebars.
It lay discarded among the bushes,
Propped up by outstretched leaves
Blooming with springtime green.
It sits there alone and nestled by nature
In absolute perfect condition.
I wonder how long it'll stay by the house
Languished and wasting away,
'Til it's rusted and soaked and unclean.
Marred by the very nature
That was kind enough to offer the bike
A new place to call its home
In the first place.

Vivid Dreams of Motherhood

The first girl was blonde; her hair soft like yours
Golden-spun yarn that rippled with light
Such youthful grey eyes, yet already she knew
What power of beauty she wielded with might

Another girl came with a head full of flames
Reminiscent, it seemed, of your kindly father
In her smile of delight, it could clearly be seen
She would grow up adored, unstifled by armour

Next came a boy who was sickly in stature
With hair like a mix of his two elder sisters'
A mellow red-gold that shone like our rings
Or the halo that matched his sprouting white wings

A third girl soon wandered to join in their fun
Sweet innocence bright in the brown of her eyes
Her laughter as warm as that first springtime
          morning
It rang as she stumbled, her hands clasped in mine

One final child, I think, is soon to come
(I imagine a boy with silken gold hair)
And complete our circle of darling creations
We await him teary without breath to spare

Come home, little one, we miss you already
Come here and spark this family alight
Come fill up our hearts 'til we're overflowing
Like a log-filled fire on a cold winter's night

Oracle

When Apollo first told me
That I could see the future
I revelled in my gift
To see beyond the world's
Bleak and miserable frame
I saw corners of the Earth
Where wonders still exist
The people there are happier
They do not cry from pain
So, I lurched into the future
And dreamed I would be
Like them some day
But Apollo's gift also
Showed me things
I wish I'd never seen
Like friendships lost
And all the thoughts
That one day would haunt me
Yet between those horrors
I still could find
A wondrous thing or two:
Four beautiful women
Who would soon be
The greatest friends
The world could offer

And a dream to be a poet
That finally came true
The future is rife
With ups and downs
A place much like the present
I have so much
To look forward to
In the years I've left to live
With Apollo's gift
I've learned to cherish
Each precious day that passes
Because who could ever truly know
What the future might bring

Chai Latte

A steaming mug of some cinnamon-flavoured drink is
watching the steady stream of people in and out of the café's
cosy interior. It's the weekend - a Saturday, if it felt like
being specific - and the café is unusually busy

The wooden table from atop which the mug watches is rickety,
rustic. Three laptops rest on its old, wrinkled surface, tipping it
this way and that as furious fingers type at a pace that almost
spills the too-hot drink from the tall, cream mug

The mug continues to steam, wondering when the woman who
bought it might take her first sip. But she is content to let it cool
as she stares at her growing essay, the hard metal of her laptop
wears at the lined wood of the uneven table

Impatient, though endlessly long-suffering, the
　　　　　　　　　　　　mug waits to be
lifted. But the woman only types faster beside her
　　　　　　　　　　　　two companions,
and perhaps they are saving the world, the mug
　　　　　　　　　　　　ponders, perhaps
she will take it with her into a new future. And
　　　　　　　　　　　　then, perhaps, she
will take her first sip.

Transition

It is now
When change is at its most potent
When life is at its most uncertain
Despite the path already paved ahead
Taunting in its firmness . . .

It is now
When dreams are given a chance
When anything and nothing at all seems possible
No matter the steady future that awaits
Dizzying in its ease . . .

It is now
When time speeds out of control
When the knowledge you've gained doesn't feel like
                              enough
Even though the tailored road is satisfied
Beckoning with its met expectations . . .

It is now that my body betrays me
Persuades me I am dividing
Plunging headfirst towards a bottom that has not
                              shown itself
And I am not tied to anything
Untethered, split into pieces

Hopes and dreams and wants spearing out in all directions
My body shuts down and I do not know which path to follow
So, I take the one that feels familiar
The one that scares me the least
The one that scares me the most

It is now

Imperfect Relief

Endless serenity
Interrupted only by
The chirp of a bird,
The fading scent of
Cigarette smoke

An expanse of
Vibrant green
Dotted with pops
Of sunflower yellow
Overlapping with
Different textures

Smooth skin
Golden-tanned,
Tattooed with
The outline of
An English flower
Creased with
Sun-cream

The ripple of
Water over tiles
Contrasting
Beige and blue

A reprieve from
The dry wind

V

THALASSA

Thalassa

I am more than an empire
I am a home
A cold, deep hearth

My heart is a mother

The gentleness in me:
It's the rippling tides,
And the innocent shallows

My soul is an empress

It's the home of terror and mystery
A spiked palace,
Whose doors have never felt a knock

My kingdom is vast
My children are strong
I am feared and I am loved

I am the queen of many waters

They Hated Her

When the girl acts as herself
True and un-smothered and unabashedly real
Then she is so effortlessly beautiful
As desirable to all as any beauty of nature could be
For when she is free and so completely unafraid,
How could she not be admired?
How could her soul not be sought after?
I would want it, would yearn for it, too
If I saw that girl dancing and frolicking in all her
                              glory,
I would love her instantly
I would be jealous of her bravery

Easier Said Than Done

Imagine you are a snake
That this skin you live in is temporary
Unfixed
It is beautifully changeable
It does not define you

Imagine the skin shedding
Falling around you in broken pieces
See the damage and pain float away,
On a wind that carries the smell of rebirth
You are new

Imagine what he did could be erased
That this new skin will take away the hurt he
                                      caused
Until you feel like yourself again
But remember,
A new skin doesn't mean a new you
It just means another beginning
Where he can no longer taint you with his greed

Just imagine you are a snake

Re-Vision

Feel oh so grateful, and thank the great goddess,
        Athena
Who in her disgust and distress gave you a blessing
        disguised as a curse
Thank the divine, heavenly woman who took such
        pity on you, dear Medusa,
That she offered, in her kindness, the gift of
        ugliness and fearfulness
So that no man could ever hurt you again the way
        her cruel uncle had done
And so that you, dear Medusa, could live out your
        days unafraid
In the gracious company of your sisters

Why Does the Princess Never Get to Save Herself?

There's one window in my high tower
It's small and glass with a pretty sill for me to sit
So I can see the world beyond the welded pane
It looks so tragically lonely without me in it
But I cannot escape my tower until someone
                decides to rescue me

There's a drop of blood on my cushioned finger
Its crimson stain keeps me alive and young
Even as I sleep a perpetual night long
My dreams are full of worlds and beauty and
                liberty
But I cannot be free until someone decides to kiss
                me

There's a fearsome dragon guarding my door
Its leathery wings block my view, and its fangs
                haunt my nightmares
This room is my only company above a world of
                flame
I long to wake and find myself nestled between
                familiar walls
But I cannot find my way home until someone
                decides to kill for me

There's cruelty and wickedness forged deep in my home
It throttles me with a world of soot and cinders
My family isn't my own, but there is no escaping their hold
The identity I seek is wrapped in the illusion of one magical night
But I cannot find my true self until someone decides to search for me

There's a prison around me where others see a palace
A keeper and oppressor where there should be a loving father
My ambition provides me a bravery I cannot truly use
I watch the melancholy world from behind gilded bars
But I cannot venture beyond until someone decides to steal me

Queen of Fire

And they feared not her power
Nor her wicked tongue
Nor her might
What they feared most of all
Was the strength of her spite
That their wounds, once inflicted
Had festered until
They had merged with her soul
A song to avenge, an order to kill
But their fear, wisely placed,
Could not foster deep courage
As men before woman,
They cowered with pleas that
Her cruelty encouraged
Lost in the heat of their craven hatred
They paved the way for
Her justice, so sacred
The call from her soul
That begged retribution
Was answered with glee
And fierce execution

Ancient Art

Her head is made of stone
With a creamy colour and granite texture
Her eyes are plain and a ghostly pale white
In her cheek lies a small chip
As though someone has hammered it away
She is un-whole and in pain
A head with no neck,
Severed by cruel nature
And dealt a lifetime of godly fame

Her lips are puckered and pink
With roughly worn patches from years of abuse
From the wind and the rain,
And the unwanted staring
Her nose is just crooked
As though she endured a great fall
And no one picked her off the ground
She is beauty on display:
A statue of patience
With a future of graceful decay

Ballad

Fear is a weapon
They use it to fight;
The people who won
And ran from the light

Wisdom is faithless
It trickles on by -
These people who jest
There's truth in their lies

Knowledge is power
Or so they do say
But the clever devour
That people's bright day

Sin is our friend
It helps forge new time
At last, a fast end
For the people who whine

All weapons are faithless
All power, our friend
Afraid, wise and clever
Our sin is pretend

The Creation of Women

It is a man's favourite hobby
To pit women against one another
To observe a girl with shrewd intensity
And weigh her worth on how different she is
To judge her ideals and desires
In comparison to the female majority
They crave our femininity to caress and mould
But expect a wife whose femininity is unique
They want to place her on a rotten pedestal
To worship her while condemning her sisters

But she was not made to be yours
She was not woven by a different thread
She was cut from the silken cloth of all women
So, treat them with the respect you offer her
Or do not speak at all

"How I Love Being a Woman"

They said they wished
their smiles were
a little more
enchanting.
I said, *me too*

They said they enjoyed
the defiant turn
of their liberating
frown.
I said, *me too*

They said they'd felt
too often
the lingering stare
of some strange
man.
I said, *me too*.

They said they loved
with all their
heart, and cried
with all their
soul.
I said, *me too*

They said they dreamt
of a time
free from fear and
haunting.
I said, *me too*

They said they adored
every daunting,
hard-earned second
of being a
woman.
I said, *me too*

Biblical Equality

We have all heard, I am sure,
Some man, at some time or another,
Assert until his last breath,
That God is a man
That this is *significant* -
Proof of some hierarchy of the sexes
God is a man; therefore, men are godly

We have all realised, I assume,
That if this stands to be true
Then surely we should, too, consider
The existence of the devil
Should we not lift his fiery loincloth
And behold his genitals?
Then we can argue with *our* final breath
That if men are godly,
So, too, are they hellish

A paradox, I daresay
Perhaps trounced by the knowledge
That, divine and genderless,
God and the devil might simply
Intend to represent two sides
Of humanity - of 'Man' or 'Mankind' -
That exist inside us all
Ever at battle

History

I was once a witch
Fiddling with my power
Like a child twirling a
Strand of her night-time
Midnight, twilight hair
Around a small finger
They burned me
My sisters, my daughters
Beneath the new moon
The fire was so bright
So harsh and so cruel
Against the calm night

I was once a mother
Holding up high my
Beautiful, golden son
At eighteen months old
He stood, already, taller
Than me and my own
A bastard, they told me
He was; I was heckled and
Beaten in my own home
They killed me for my
Indiscretion: my father
My uncle, it made an

Impression, my screams were
So blunt, so dreadfully dull
Against my father's sharp
Blade as it pierced my skull

I was once a Queen
With blood on my hands
How cunning, they said
What I did to that man
My husband, the king, no
More, no more, I wanted
It, I needed it: more, more
Give me more - I relished, I
Feasted: a lioness downing
A deer for her cubs, they were
Not grateful, they hunted me
On one of my hunts, the blood
Was so red, so dirty, so dead
Against the white of my
Shirt as they took me to bed

I was once a whore
Touching and touched in
Places so dark and
Uncomfortably sore, all to
Feed the ones I left that
Morning at home
The ones in need, so

I did the deed, for the
Good, I let them spill
Their hateful seed
They loved me then, for
The body I learned to use
So well, they savoured the
Swell, its sweet, sweet smell
So far we would go, I would
Cry, I would plead, because
I knew how they liked to
See me bleed, I let them
Do everything, do anything
At all, they thought they were
Kind, they thought I would
Fall; 'no', how dangerous a
Word to be said, it fell from
My lips, so they cut off my
Head, my hands were so small
So childlike against the broadness
Of their fully-grown chests

She Adapts; She is Trapped

A wolf in a den of dogs
She does not belong
She is untamed
She is free - is she?

She listens, she watches
She learns their ways
She learns to sit
She learns to stay
She learns to choke down
Their dry food and suppress
The urge to kill
And chase her prey

Feminism

There was not suffrage nor suffer-age
for the sake of pungent equality
They did not line up and pile up and rile up
to have their identities ripped away
Those nuances that were cherished,
even as they'd been used to force us under,
no one wanted them to dwindle in number
We were never meant to become the same,
they did not fight just so we would continue
to feel that belabouring pain
Under a guise of equality, of justice,
when we needed *equity* to right those years of
malice
They did not wish for us, who we are, to be wiped
clean,
forced to dull to a masculine gleam
Just because we want *fair* does not mean we want
indistinguishable, blended selves
A battle-wound bloody, an ugly tear:
healed and sealed brutally, efficiently, but without
care or concern for the scar it might leave
The horrid, too-sweet equality it might try
to convince us has been conceived
But suffrage is endless and suffer-age is life
There will be no equity one day without a past,
a present rife with strife

VI

THEMIS

Puppet to Society

If you pull my strings, I will jump for you
I will bend to your will until my limbs turn numb
and fall off
If you tug too hard, I won't cry out in pain or
resistance
I will grit my teeth and bear it unknowingly
If you jerk me left and right, I will follow your
orders
I will move with a fluid grace that seems like my
own
If you wrench tears from me, I will cry and choke
I will sob until my eyes are filled with sand
If you urge me to smile, I'll laugh with desperate
glee
I will grin until my muscles clench and scream in
agony
If you tell me what to feel, I will mould my
thoughts for you
I will put my heart and soul into that emotion
If you tell me I'm free, I will believe you
I will never call myself your puppet

Ouroboros

Hidden things -
Revealed in sudden
Glaring reality
By a shaft of
Sunlight that
Glitters and bends
Sneaking between
Shadows and wisps
Forcing out the
Truth, no matter
How painful.

Painful things -
Soothed and tended
To by a touch so
Featherlight it
Almost seems to be
A dream that
Leaves you with
Questions and
Queries that bring
Sweat to your
Sweet lips.

Unanswered things -
Maddening in

Their adamant
Secrecy and deception
Disallowing anyone
To shed light
On the truth
Assassins of reality
And of revelation
Remaining in the
Ever-present dark
Without consideration
For those deserving
The freedom
That accompanies
Knowledge.

The Cult of Eros

To be in love means to be blind
As the embrace tells us:
a depiction of Psyche and her husband
So brilliant to her virginal eyes, they would
never again look upon another
Blinded by love before she could search
further beneath its thin surface

You have been blinded much the same
by the pretty face that sprouts words
of peace and unity, while changes to
the constitution are made behind
your trust-turned back; you never
knew that trust should be
earned, not taken forcibly from the hands
of a blind man who only
wanted to be loved the way he loves
But he loves too foolishly and too
shallowly, as Psyche did
Now you suffer at the cruel hands of
the object of all your impetuous desires

Tragedies Unforgotten

I didn't know you,
But they did
I didn't watch you,
But he did
I didn't love you,
But she did

Yet even though these things are true
Once I knew you,
I cried for you
Once I knew you,
I mourned for you
I mourned for them, too

You are angels now
And you see me mourn
You see me write for you,
Remember you
You are no longer unknown
By me, by the many
Now you are unforgotten
Your tragedy is our history,
Our past

And they will miss you,
They will not forget you

White Gold

22
In 1 year, if I wanted to be like her
I would find myself bound in white gold
I used to want to be like her, I did, I did, I did
Now I am not so certain, how young she was to be
                        so sure

Oh yes,
I want to be like her: be sincere, be brave, be sure
I want to be like her, even after she'd walked
              through that church door
Beyond shone her imagination
Her creation, her innovation
Bound then, in white gold, she did not let her
              touch rot and grow old
She did not sell her words or let them be sold

For years
I questioned the politics of her intention
Older, I was confused by the lack of prevention
She did not tire of her role,
It did not weary her old-fashioned soul
I wanted to be like her, just the same
To find a new language, to find a new name

But no,
My judgement, my shame, they turned out to be
                                      wrong
I thought she'd given up her mind for that song
Its melody is heaven, it tempted me too
I felt ashamed, I thought she knew
But I want to be like her, who never gave up
With every friend, every life, with every "fuck"

Bound
In white gold, her eyes were not haunted
Her feet were not tired, her mind not unsorted
There are birds and tigers in her home
With them she is free, she is never alone
Unbound and unburdened, I realise now
White gold is not cruel, it is simply a vow

22
I can wait, we need not be the same
I no longer fear losing myself when I find a new
                                        name
When I find a new house and make it my own
There'll be birds, there'll be tigers that talk on the
                                        phone
My politics cannot be tied down by white gold
I will write 'til forever, 'til I'm old, so, so, old

Important Choices

There is pollen in my throat
It chafes and scratches
There is pollen in my eyes
Rub, rub, rub
Until they swell and seal shut
Until they are trickling salt
Until they are weighed down
With phantom irritants
There is pollen in my nose
That makes it itch
That makes me sneeze
That makes it run with
Snot and blood and I cannot
Stop the incessant bleed

Take your antihistamine!
Cure what ails your face
Claritin will clear your
Running, bloody nose
We promise you'll feel
A-ma-zing!
Fexofenadine will fix
The itch in your eye
Relieve that swell and

See clearly again!
          For your throat, Benadryl
Will say 'begone!'
Be rid of that scratch before
It's stayed long
You can trust us
We promise to solve all of
Your summertime problems
We only have your best interests
At heart

But Claritin cannot stop
My throat from scratching
And Benadryl will not keep
My eyes from swelling
Fexofenadine will not reverse
The blood from my nose
I don't know, I can't choose
I have lived with hay fever
All my life
Now I see it can never be
Entirely vanquished

Forced Taxonomy

For You, I cannot speak
Nor for Him or for Them
Only for Us am I permitted
To share spoken thoughts
For the We and the She

But, perhaps, for Them
I can write, I can anguish
I can bleed upon the
White, white paper of
Our contemporary history

Perhaps, for You, for Them
For Him, for Us, for We
For She, I am permitted
To ponder, not aloud, but
With ink, just how we all
Connect? History just won't
Seem to let us

Now

"Nothing can make it better.
Nothing can make it right."

"*But isn't it better that we are trying,
that we want to make it right?
Would you rather we just pretended
it never happened at all?*"

"I would prefer it to have never
happened at all."

"*We cannot offer you that. You ask
too much. We cannot rewrite history.*"

"But you can undo it? Is that what
you believe?"

"*We can make it right.*"

"It will never be *right.*"

"*Then we can stop it from happening
again by acknowledging it wasn't okay.*"

"It is already happening again. I see
it every single day."

"We are trying our best."

"Try harder."

"We cannot skip to the future. You ask too much."

"There is no future. There is only the present."

A Living Corpse

Go on, go
Faster, faster
Down down down
Straight down the
Mountain, go
        shoos shoos shoos
Keep going, down
Towards certain death
Towards oblivion
Towards-
DON'T STOP!
. . . .
Is she . . . is she okay?
Of course she is
Get up, go on
You don't need
A beating heart
To ski, go on, go
Faster, faster
Down down down
Straight down
The mountain, go

Unfounded Prejudice

Dear Pluto
So altered by the
Romans who
Grew bored of
Your dreary
Complexion

You have lived
A life in
Heavy disquiet
Rejected by
Your ever-present
Companions

Who refused to
Call you their
Friend, their kin
When earthly
Beings so callously
Defined

Your frozen home
As Other, different
Smaller than
Theirs in worth

And always
Untrustworthy

I Do Not Have a Lion's Heart

A man with a lion's heart
Praised for his courage
King of the modern jungle
Powerful, infallible, unquestioned

A woman with an antelope's heart
Tentative and shrewd
Daring to drink at the watering hole
Braving the lion's bite
For the sake of her young
For the sake of her survival

She was born to be prey
The king hungers for her flesh
He corners her, teeth bared
A show of deadly power
Honed in his muscles
Earned through a rule of fear

She goes down fighting
Her calves' bellies full of water
As she dies, she asks herself:
Who was really brave in the end -
The lion or the antelope?

Genocide

A zealot, prepared to kill for his cause
A child, forced to die far away from home

A fanatic, sacrificing her own people for the sake of
 her pride
A doctor, resigned to taking lives for her people's
 sake

A soldier, unwaveringly loyal, disgustingly cruel
A grandmother, willing to sacrifice her life so
her family will not be held back by her extra weight

A world leader, turning a blind eye
A father, holding his screaming daughter, skin
blackened beyond recognition, as she dies

A family, begging everyone, *anyone*, for aid
A celebrity, claiming they cannot speak out because
they are not well-enough informed

A people, dying and burning en masse
for the crimes of the few
A people, far away, prosperous, sympathetic as they
turn off the news

Poetry Has Power

In a café somewhere in
the depths of London,
there is a young woman
trying to write poetry
about politics. Yet despite
living in a world where
tragedy seems to be
closing in on all sides,
shading hope in humanity
like an eclipse, the words
will not flow. No matter
how hard she tries. No
matter how far she plunges
into the ocean of empathy
that stretches to a
cavernous pit in her gut.
Writer's block frequents
her café table at the
strangest times. It leaves
the important things unsaid.